Copyright © 2023 by NSN-CC, LLC
Mr. Pickles as depicted in this book is the unique and exclusive property of NSN-CC, LLC.

Published by Long Overdue

All rights reserved. No part of this publication may be reproduced, distributed, or transmitted in any form or by any means, including photocopying, recording, or other electronic or mechanical methods, without the prior written permission of the author and illustrator, except in the case of brief quotations embodied in critical reviews, sharing photos of the book on social media, and certain other noncommercial uses permitted by copyright law. For permission requests, please contact the publisher at chris@longoverduebooks.com

> "It's the things we play with and the people who help us play that make a great difference in our lives."
>
> **Fred Rogers**

> To my family & friends who inspire, encourage, and make a great difference in my life.
>
> **Vicki Sheaffer**

> "Go where you are celebrated, not where you are tolerated."
>
> **Patricia Koznick**

> To all the people who have believed in my creative talents and helped me succeed. Thank you!
>
> **Chanda Cook**

PICKLEBALL

It's a Big Dill!

A Slice of History with a Little Relish

www.longoverduebooks.com

MOVE over tennis, ping-pong, and badminton

A new game's takin' over from St. Paul to Britain

What began long ago to fill time

Has drawn from the

SPORTS to combine

Now **EVERY** city and town has a court

PICKLEBALL!
Has become an international sport

So, how did this come to be?

Well, here's a little slice of **HISTORY**

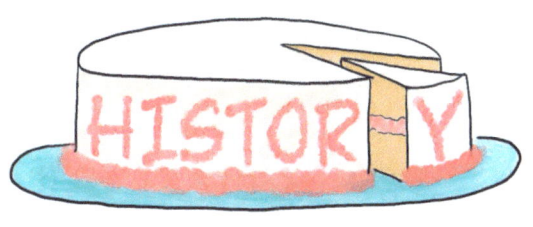

Returned to Pritchard's home
To find his family with

"BORED"
syndrome

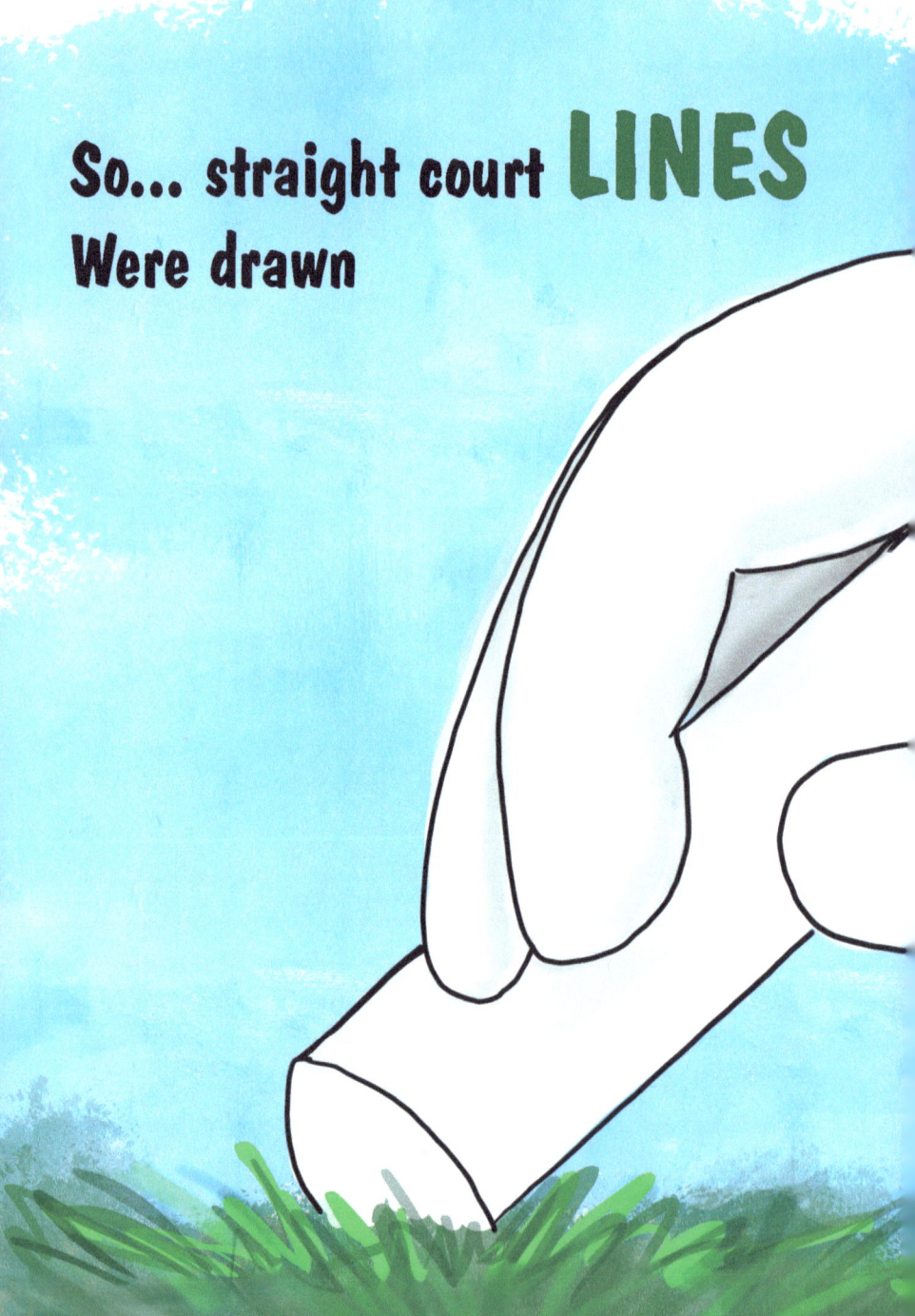

So... straight court LINES
Were drawn

A little improv went a **LONG** way

and everyone was encouraged to play

With small net and plastic ball

they started to volley one and **ALL**

From the Littles
to the **GRANDS**
they rallied with paddles in hand

It was so much fun!
They LAUGHED by default

then moved the game to the hard asphalt

Underhand serves and **BOUNCES** were better

Barney, the neighbor, joined in to write up the rules with a **SPIN**

A new **SPORT** to be played
on equal ground.
Such a clever pastime
they had found!

Olives, relish, and peppers were JEALOUS

For the name "PICKLES" the Founders were zealous

Now it's a name we'll **NEVER** forget!

Across the **WORLD** every day there's a tourney, Pritchard, Bell, and ol' Barney started the journey

They're all in the
PICKLEBALL
Hall of Fame

memorialized forever
by their name

It's more than the "Game of the Day"
PICKLEBALL
is here to stay!

Let Pickleball fans find you!

Re-order Book Here

@itsabigdillpickleball

It's A Big Dill - Pickleball

Entirely Bonkers Media Co

So Darn Creative

Author Vicki Sheaffer

Tennis on Selby

Pine Tree Apple Orchard

Contact us at itsabigdillpickleballbook@gmail.com to add yours!

"Sport has the power to change the world, it has the power to inspire. It has the power to unite people in a way that little else does."

Nelson Mandela

www.ingramcontent.com/pod-product-compliance
Lightning Source LLC
Chambersburg PA
CBHW041723070526
44585CB00001B/15